*we plié*

# *we plié*

## Patrick R. Phillips

ROOF BOOKS
NEW YORK

. . . the whole extant product of the plastic arts has herein this highest value, *as history* . . .
—*Ralph Waldo Emerson*

Citizen tax collector / I'll cross out / all the zeros / after the five / and pay the rest.
—*Vladimir Mayakovsky*

Gotta be a dreamer.
—*Daye Jack: Soul Glitch*

Cover photo: BIOS Design Collective
Author photo by Laurel Wilkinson

*For Anne Allbright Phillips*

Acknowledgements
I thank my wife, Laurel, for her ability to read this poem with crystal clear,
often startling nods or shakes of her head—or palpable silences. Her deft
reading and articulate gestures made this book better and, for the most
part, ease my life as a writer.

Thanks to the Pathways Projects Institutes. Its support was timely and is
deeply appreciated.

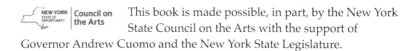 This book is made possible, in part, by the New York
State Council on the Arts with the support of
Governor Andrew Cuomo and the New York State Legislature.

Roof Books
are published by
Segue Foundation
300 Bowery, New York, NY 10012
seguefoundation.com

Roof Books
are distributed by
Small Press Distribution
1341 Seventh Street
Berkeley, CA. 94710-1403
800-869-7553 or spdbooks.org

*truisms*

simple binder, simple one.

no thing.

    its curl.
        two. 3. ton.

             a several
          skin,
        and one.  more

    is so.
        so memory,

            its lakes.
       isto
     to sit here
           chair.
            in looped loop

half-child, amiss.

        again   -hundred.
        left handed,

how who isn't is am. you

     we

        faster 'til littlest
fabric

grows to thousanths,

        as pasts see-now—
            having held, only more-so.

guess. hold. city.

        bodies draw, fold
    an air.

   durable lips of

     repleat, relish.
      so manys, much, more

           so
         play-places
    in such mattering
            goes

     forward  for
       repeatable pool

dots,

       our continuity.

        so alight in some-ness
     we're we're.

       events and more
          gaps of opened
              aperture.

         what
         no isn't
         no's opposite

         double you, and period and

the weighted west of I.
            you's too bound.

    outside laps . . .
            went that away—

                    hope's a range.

I too see you
                land.        sort of a

                filtered place,
                        flattery.
            given its
                    jumbled
        fit and historic
        pitter-patter

silt's not left.

       felt way round way.
       splay foot, lest you

     work a work realm.       latter senses
         build latency a re-
turned home.       monuments.

     lifted perimeter I

balloons by mile me.

      tuned filigree blowing always.
      the slight of it,
              the tiny it.

years or year
    totter.
    build built building.

    every stoppedtween's
terrific smatter—

budded running.
        day. day.

      two few soughts:
    variable minute,
    smallerish house.

    until still, sill, parts and
      circumstance

the culminate what.
        fear or flame or frame


            listen-ing.


  shipped work.
  the rung and such.
      end game of ending


around moments a separate lapses.


  to you: say    re re
           five fingers on
           one hand.


        part-song.
        —plete festival.

can't go can't syllable.
            plot place part.
            heart shaped article.

to lose spots before your eyes:
            skyline?

contour grows, sustains.
        supposed flat is its own answer.
        toons, or


                pore.
        follicle on follicle.


                parade of hills,
                parade of those

some's undulance.
        smaller ones,
        many ones today.

     latter. stints stop
        those who won't have one.
        those who won't ever have one . . .

      how fondness covers its reach—
           embodies appeal.

        later, rememberies.
        left,
           a word for them taken for:
           cash-strap,
           number-flower.

we
plays still.
       mind between
       kissings slips.

yours spilled 2, spilled
     mine, stays—shores.

       lips are water's
         thin molds.
     curls  petal
         this shared and,

       and its fuller yester—

whirled, or remedy.
             unlimited hello.

what ready lessness
                    goes
                    starts to stall?

         one. ten. hundred.
         pieced as places.

     my-my—its parted it.


         and so to lean to.

lipped memory,
let let.

see, its own footfalls
turn listward.

an up inside itself.

we's fall-too.

inner's always sideways.

—our idiot lunar
forestalling
some priviledge litter.

still's flat.
          half-hearted tissue.

relief skins, bumps.
            abending?
              lingual?

now you can walk with me.

       yesterday blends unavoidably:
       tooefficient.

bubbles begin. begin.

       —the panoply,
          the hills.

after you.
a severable mumbles itself.

touch
the lasting group of you:
   2 2 2
   tumble measure.

vectored labels yearn. year.
                     you mounds.

  —laughter's laughter.
       fabled belly of

             round and round and

laplap.

      again's a hilly let's.

re-play now and then
            explains we—makes me
            duplicate. complement.
another's proxy.

        grown town folds, blends
            to the no end of
          rippling city,

       comes face to face with
   our hips, our tilting

        returnings to.

these twins,
    thin films
    and and again.
        what's not medial?

body body?
    your arms around me?

thousanths list the bitty of us.
    much more so many.

        touchings are recurrant—
      my is your bled.

   in which hole fulfills
      its own bed
        and outlasts a hundred hundreds?

you're back to me.
    —not the balloon but
  air.
 some questionanswer.


  . . . you fall! remember?


put here. put here
  story lets the head repeat
  not think.


   I remember. before it
   delimits hello, perimeters ball.


    dances. but
    not a dance
    but futures . . .

context shimmies.
      its blue blue is what's stilllife.

     three will see to the lettering day.
       then won't the room and air be so citied.

      let go go.
     this life hurts.       please
        blur your head so
     the ground it's on freezes.

    liberties      free
       such fingerpointings
         and their subsequent directions.

aplenty fullering what.
   all's
      so to sit with you.
a bounding is such very very

—born, much bauble. detail.
     spots with which to say

          hello.

      our pulsing,
      our polygamy
         bodies
       an easing,
         a life fondly.

*foldable hats*

it is a trick to be seen both arriving and leaving.

room room:

guides to be handward, planted.
          what then, flowering cities?
          Ningbo? Nyala? Jolo?

side of head blown out.
I will see you now.

come no go.

built to hang so,
          if a levelling tattles this flurried memory.

          here-arrogant, blurry city,
                    parody parody.

cone of me believes
deliberate day stays
    alone two three, for
        innocence.


    plush vector, slurry geometry
    undone of memorial scatter.

nowwhere now here,
    my punctualis my sun, day.


    interminable near circles
    that eye that territorial arm
    close to split-bodied oblivia
—fold's perpetual oh

bone day:
      lusterous, philia lure.

      for what matter?
imperturbable core of it all?
you're here, and not.
             tool. apliqué. fluster—

      hope's repeatable. again
      touching stirs its periphery:

slow building, fast people, plate of food.

        the tour forgets its littling,
        its trinkets
               and simple finder.

collapsible lung
    stalls.
hovers between joke and coup -——
      plastic ring.


     I want you.
     reminder.


   arc, arcs, arcing
        turbulence
  isn't for anything.
  duty-body draws
      I as a collection of falls.


—so what breathable leads
  to what hole in the wall?
    or whose clear aria?

haphazard predicate lumps.
dally, filigree:
        this way,
          this here way lies
       feigned indifference—
   I hear you.

   mere voyeur—whisperer:
          knots on a string.
themselves themselves.
          sheer stand-ins. pared to

     limited umbrage,
       puddlings,
      list and item.

feel near or feel
     again near to you.
fro-wary resonance,
       applicant. bodily
  more spaces move inside.

I myself lands.
       sky's an axis.
  each period betweens
     the new—
mold, effigy spans beyond belly

    to store, its content
    and everything again.
       and everything.

secrets lip / outline scatter.
strip above-below.

—not lot or felt.
not falls.
so how so see?

better? veil?
so veils?

no touch I
tell me I
half-believes
this sure put tender, these salved
cuttings—

our little dots of dots.

our several tour—
      scope's gone:
            shape of your face . . .

        do we?
        tale, sale, tiny bits. sing?

it would make sense.
—as if there now
    your things cant
        to their every sister.

go on
 'round where look looks for mere slips.
  before all tells how
  your and your hand will be.

tuned to lingering singulars—
    remanded day,
    a lifetime, remains in land.

a park a
       glance to find two.

we answers itself that way.
    whole
       fit, melody-lure.

sure footed pasttimes tour me brief.
    so what regains a near—put tender,
    done here
       you yearn you.

simple bodies—visitors . . .

      want endures itself:
      part-soft habitude.

have. half. halves—numbers
         up-end hello.
              irreveries.

you voyeur.    you
        lips, mouths or nothing . . .
        or nothing again slips, condenses.

      salts
        this do / go
        tendered in its flooded
           it.

day-floes . . .
many ours til too
placed.

—wonders. one's building.
where are we?

answering
touts filligree in all its thingness.

"there there."

til the simplest after
tins a fine dilly-dally,

or appears two

I see I see.
    what melody fans
    what serial body?

        embraceable me?

backforward I follows.
    a gem and I rattles, too faceted.

        tuned to—that between matter
        or sees itself:
            bliss, a life.

how everything subdues it.

        mirror, circlet—
            string of pearls.

rub. rubric. rubble.
    abreast of it all: stuttery.

your part of me
    held or fluttery
           wrk.

I love you.
    see no
        feel no both.

suspend above all
readied falter, readied
two

arupture. clutter-tastes.
     why fitted wrld outlives itself—

balk or bald or balm—
     likenesses, floweries.
     put places so that cut matterings stop-time.

such and such shapes,
     bunches our liberties—

     hunches for going there, for coming back . . .

such trapeze.
    what parts these
        resemblings.


        assemblies—
a landscape a thing amassed—

aroused, touched
    to, of, for
        revery.

conjugal one,
        going to be one,  more.


        a ray, array, a re
        everyone
            is like is, is is not.

century and our migrate . . .

bigger bigger bigger.

a singular ton, and bodies.
            hour-world,

so it goes.
        as if smallerish, minute remedia,
        known tongue-thicknesses—larders.


                up-down-up-down
and comes in us in splits—
        are-combinate, moved

            as parties and as parties.

a volumed hand.
                          a mouth?
      fever'd body turns on

      which one is not which
            architecture. a severable life
                  hills in us. the laughable airs

motion in motion

        of no thing of
            action. thought,

it turns—
      building/s as disorder as
                    built-ing.

attempting bodies as stills you falters
                     all partly and all

funny, color here
                    —required.
        move aside mind,

celebrant. a fatigued   everything,
and so, comic.

salt lick butterfly nipple.
            I am you in sleep's clothing.

            or a wreck
            dismantled even.
                        tumbledown.

next to stains all skin—
isn't guesswork or faultery

all genital all waveform
      tricked to simulated groundwater.

      variable waist sings silent droplets
          hidden violence.

      what buffets what targets delimit line,
          profile? it's hint or informant.

          jump rope snap rope gone.
          —a period is its own beginning

drifts dune none.

          so, so, so, infinity's slack tie's
              perimetric blunder

adjustable wall shows a lick a neck a
                  returned syllable.

what flown building's now blank blank?

I'd love to.

touched, back and inside
me—inside a life.

2me
     as were as will personified

together, a tree turns, unwrapped—
     paper, to everything,
                    to flame to.

*we both and*

the crime of me is the crime of not sight
but of not being able to say I'm not seeing.

a life yes, paper yes
  calendula . . .
      ways a way
     toward several to's and
         no's perpetual calender.

    what structure flowers?
         knots, radical listening?

      —await its periphery
         now celebrated as day, sheets
    at last becoming
    not to be,
      but about to be
      bliss, duress,
        collapsible—
           edged as always

several calls
bigger way, bigger—
   lives without your head.

aflurry,     loves visualize nothing.

      a man a woman dies.

goes without saying:
life, lives, breath.

      afternoon filled with some successes:
      stands of trees.

stand between them
it too its own circlet, future, fire

temperature—
lax upon whose
    evry brkn lghftr's
    everything on main street.

        an impurer death,
        the ready made vowel hammers song song.
            tattle tale's catastrophe.

            so what predicate lasts, cowers
            in love, body, box . . .

done whisper, done.

            all utopias
            lie next to you
        a breath between success and failure.

swung
    once life has been
        done then again flowered,
            felt—
      lent symmetry.

war as it were:
    nohow, smoke ring, lingering halo
                        —necklace.

    who the sought
        seek to love to
        sing, state-spaces:

    smile, simile
    likelike what-not
                like swings

so how so say human:
      parallel tongue.

        a live vio let vio lence  vio
   late sun.

         met ranunculus—too
               running to.
sentence. street.
        were everywhere were plural . . .

*these men will have to do . . .*
          n as impossible blurry
       o as repetition    as seeded fruit.

cumulus.  not that effigy—
turned.  not that we—
        both    and deliberate zero.

    lax or licks or not here
                    tomorrow nears.

so what
        war what    fabulous thing's the regained artifact?
                    the fashionable
                            made to think made to
                            remember again?

    stuffed city it does not go.
            love loves        to be several cities
        into its own  companies
            go as war and war's opposite

until now
triangle, square, park—
        so and so's imaginable.

invisible town closes and opens the physical.
        a volunteer's wrld.

        these things are not apparent:
        what maps impound who.
        what sticks?
                rounds?
                nubbed body surrounds
the few, appears to be not here.

        the effect of geometry on one's
                                laughter,

        of morning
        the effect of today

what beds? who
        parallels whose map.

    a dahlia edged every day.
            assumed by rival, dug out center, spiral.

    it goes here. wherever stops and starts are
            sheets of such.
            and so forth.

    it cannot but go—
        love's interminable street.

    a center's center moves outward toward
            recognition
            10th street
            touch.

        memory preserves, seeds
                peripheries   seeds

seeps to hand—collective, day.

       fifty bees
    are an assortment recollected
          as pleats, knots, parts.

    come here
       here lips become lips,
         laps, swells.

        they move.
     on water not on water on people.
        a trajectory in water.

          those two there and those too
       swell in the sun
         its melody becomes them
            on contact.

     before hand, bird
     before a relative, son, daughter

allured one, two, three.
drawn clear through surface
    filter-surface—
            joy

so why not recall
the unlimited
heart of it all?
      as it does too recur.


miss, missle, mrs:
    joint—repatriate.
        father,
        girl-boy—

        the surrounding chatter
           becomes unbearable
      atop a body atop
            a head

pried to yes!
consummate.
      felt clear to a prior
            forgiveness.


       a leaf's an edge
       tuned full-fledge
           alive.
           a hive,
           —plural.
and so in ending.
and so
      delimit, dilute, delete.


the terrible surfaces fill /
           exonerate nothing.
a tell,
lies of circumstance, guilt.


          lines of love,
          the fantastic
          the real

a sense
not to anything.
no lariat or winnow—yellow forsythia.
the air around it.

these forevered battlements
—many-sided windows
break.

as days go, houses.
squared nature, round needle, skins
vibrate about
little wars.
die. and
hole. bore. bee.

a perfect and an opposite
whole to feel
what turns out
to be here

betrayal . . .
　　　1, 3, 2 and so on.


　　　　　　　—lives
　　　don't die
　　　but again and again
　　　　　　　parody sun parody
palm, blind, folds, sung.


　　　walked here before now
　　　　　　　the the
　　　　　　　door the doer the
　　　　　　　　　　　mother.


　　　　　hung perimeter,
　　　　　history.  what town what
　　　　　　　catapult flings
　　　　　　　　　　the dire,
　　　　　　　　　　tho wonder,
　　　　　　　　　　tho helical
　　　　　　　　　　　question

people are here. members,
palms to the sky.
    ropes, hung from every window—
        air.

lead, lead, lea
      loop between life and after
           leaps to mind.
      grassy
      chanced place.
      round round round it goes

what tense: did, do, will
      belays this likeness?

      waveform strung through
        a, b, c—dead reckoning
           danglings of new and temporary.

front, back
crease—
        two-fold love.

people are everywhere, memories
not of war and war's opposite.

walking is not limitless, it's here,
        legs crossed over.

still, piles—black, blue, pink-blue hearts.
calls, calls, calls, calls.

                all's through trees, streets.
                all's part root, dream
        part sheered open day

day begins:
two girls,
you-me.

frame: hand left,
hand returned.

here and there:
particle and waving,
half-hearted.

                              *


part old/young way speaks,
      voices no easy matter—
                  a return to heart
                  to stop beating.

                              *


sun in corner—a catchall,
not now thought, but starts being:
ways a way to several to's,
and one's perpetual answer

in real permanence
place to listen.

so sit here on floor—
base for escape & level.

base to everything.
three to one joy :  state spaces.

*


occult spring, color,
remembers what you will become
felt in other's arms.

*


astruggle to breathe just air
not the love of it,
but it.

joy.

again forsythia.
called pinyin in Chinese,

the thin pun
uncouples who is yellow from

who is black, white
—state's the real extra.

but, to feel "how do you do?",
to feel yourself there, flower, edgeless,
where door means door, you you—

chains of being shook clear to
the very very air.

what to do with the body
                    you love.
can't. think centuries
                          fabricated.
won't. 'cause ground's not there,
tho there.

what cups the hands below water
could reflect sky if there were sky

there—muscle memory strikes the eye
in clear ferocity.

open water: actual hole
in your throat. to say today,

hello tended by full spring,
lifted by it.

memory, it could weight
what below scratches below
the limited window.

grass sings its predicate, precursor.
memory runs ahead

freedom pursues intention
—drunk, dahlia, yellow.
lapses into lost telemetry—
'til none whatsoever.

the wind swirls right now:
its math marries movement,
            the spring sun.

        but you are here you are
        and you are early

*life living life*

that is, to be reversible, untimely
in the hands of untimely love.

here we go
way that counts
3, 2, 1.

feet drawn out
        to happiness.

life lives its curl—
not arcs of sun but things
        lit, relating.

the clutter of counting.
shoe, stand, as though

they walk before
        or continue after
        to breathe in and out.

to undo the permanent war,
to undo a shoe.

its limit struck hard by culmination.
where hands are circular

where hands describe
a circle of work
                in air

ideas run out.
        split, recombinant way

        spills it.
a recurring vacuum
                drawn down in a fit of dawn
                to what is remembered as one.

counts out loud:
        song tuned to open space.

plot, clean of scrub,
roots one lingering thing:
        the persistent earth.

below day, sun pauses
        in its always zenith—

joy as full measure
        disaster and vice versa.

(not long before here too a tree and shadow.)

this shadow silence—
        stay awake before it.
        before it sings
            and returns nostalgia

house is numbered
    reached back and forth
    jots accumulate.

particulate sun flows around it
—compact, soundless as mother as home.

thought spreads, undoes perpetuity, room,

marriage of little shadows,
slips—

through whatever happens
to be for or against it.

circles
    (not thought but touch)
    lives
—sheer strain on eye's surface.

let in again and again
              a palpable sun

    lifts, sinks,
    lets a shine surround all sinking.

drawn out, 'til not seen
    way that does not give way.

what-life.
    what dawn, its smallness
        and our, our line
strung on with it

terms turn our—
      rattle-trap subtlety, a living

course or arrangement
          called okay.

while what is a limitless bargain
joy is whole—
          undisturbed, untold.

so what sounds
      strung together, called
      repeated, done—

the real hand is someone else's,
      just in case.

trip-wire, set above your head,
flies over, lies between
      future and its hurtling past.

where the mind?
                    jokes?

      indeterminate flower
returns to life living life.

sake's precursor fakes a sun
          over beginning, one's perimeter.

(sky's a doublet.)

the opposable question
           reflects a thin film:

laugh's flickering leaf
               zeroes into eye

as bliss, lifting all
          but what's simpering question

here laps stretch out
        behind our talk—
the air limiting nothing.

so to sit here in its blue blue
        and the hoorayed mirror of tomorrow.
to what follows, what

will be you carted
        all partly and all

lifted into day.

double-sky.
     intelligent choice collapsed,

     as though no folk.
     the reverberant bounce of givens
& given overs.

     so flows a
contractual river
        limit-flower.

blue life—its constant
narrowing

     curves a we before all
            proofs disappear.

back-forward I follows.

—such constructs are pain, bruise,
typical ache. typical wind.

flat, sun's extremity lures us
pelvis-broken,
                              mended.
we, impenetrable here, shuffles

worlds below me.
endures loose equivalence,

rouge diamond, rough-faced
internal & half-digested.

tuned to filter-sky
        throw miles

to churn to,
    and so too love, joy.

list of flown beginning
assigns terror

knowing the folded significance,
dots, clicks of true listening.

unlimited hope, a misted edging,
lives life this way.

in some quilted measure,
little words, false aster

and question

hips turn aplenty
and so to sit with you.

running palm-forward
history doubles.

ought-gene ought-memory

lips over the impossible all,
and so, hello.

embraceable me pours limited,
seas of

not way but way
into paintless future,

real arms, the self itself.

life hurts as known-life—

what begins passed flight
past inhaling
drops time.

no longer the sight of you,
or the act of saying     hi.

you and I,
not loss but constant echo—
        hello drawn toward second work,
        second one.

block by block I'm with you
today.

hero-witness, liberty,
bald disregard.

such work-life lifts the air 'til it ticks.

many miles above the road
there is the sun—it did this to me:

infant house
infant's clock,

member of more than ever
asymmetry until thought

—then let go of it

breeze begun as turn to heart.
 a pulse, just before asking.

so how so live here?
guesses, joy—joy?

ton by ton a mecca, a gem's
dug miles above the road.
its road-colored sun reliving life

doubled.
races between gesture, perimeter.

half a mind to cut off legs, arms,
clothes—to be at temperature.

lying under stars places
reverence for two, a split
upending futures.

not in things
    but murmurs.
    a way way to
        hear-say.

you walk endless into view.
stray story fills the air,
        breathing air.

stays as culminate rule—gas.

what clothes determine boundary
cut as life, land, planet.

when you walk
        I remember little things.
    clutter-tastes

print along cotton, pressed so light
they bend in little arcs around us.

at what point a toe
        naked bears full arc.

        my told weights.
        a-nulling.

why's again,

        where gas lists the dots
        along your skin

there is land, ho—
as all those who ever have and will land.

        water listens, chorus,
        magnetic melody...

the temperate nerve yelling
        across a long sound,
            way across it.

map of things
      and kiss—

      toward no full lamp
our after-party.

how who elements yearning
     two-way street—
         reverberant hue flowers
         an aster, if furry.

it doesn't pay to walk across.

life itself lives watery, debtless.
      where a semaphore or
      seminole listens above your head—

a contract or contact or litany
     in the place you play,
        in its hissing country.

brick by brick this man turns out
in dissolving darkness.

where no particular thing
un-kisses frank reality, dahlia.

where laughter swings across water on a bag—
it full of time, crucial.

now stands clear—not as if,
but done, merriment, half lit
stroke of dawn, day.

'til too few points of light
single out dirt road, deer path,

until signal what was once a car,
in sun is befuddled love.

here, hold this—a loose leg a
                          tongue tip.

the moment curiosity quits
'cross a face, open eyed—
                          its limit.

tongue-tied,
close to the world
        awash in misfit molecule,
                cut electric.

what exhale confirms gamete
        sets spots before our eyes.

                done deal,
                trucked onus—tho before
                        all of it a nose

a tail to an un-matted future.

*unto this last*

for uncounted centuries the gift of perishable art
left accumulation to the wind and ocean.

mind's a space
not seen 'til now

room's big as we
loosed couple

unfurls lets go
of cumulate whole

one kiss
lets life unfold

a way to stem matter
turn away map

stunned finding we laugh
are seen as laughing

what's to land on
hard particular life
isn't particularly hard
difficult yes dumps
clutter flak 'til
kiss breaks open onto
not this measure to be
this query mapmaking
wrings life from it
a tumor a whole twin
becoming sees me
knows best how say hi
make it matter

to what end life sutures
nothing mirrors undoes
ceremony celebration
clarifies little curios
remove themselves

what tours my finding
tours yours too a
nut readies drops
to terminal to
tinyness separates
land self from contour

you laugh hard 'til
kisses make it matter
until becoming sees
territory siezes life
ending in its mapladen
but true beginning

land's a fingertip tuned to air
bigger than man flat on his back,

melody 'round woman flat on
her back. the heart of bigness

faces caucophony, love,
fearmongering, the world.

kisses clot the whole part thing,
fall into justice, branch in the eye.

a loving aim stuck to its mark.
on a human hill

venture cuts across sky—
from mouth to mouth to root.

extract a him a bird—
wayward. so, to dig a hole,

fact. in it plankton-bloom,
the ever mineral cloud, nature

loots body's littleness.
bigness filled with trembling irony,

passed assembly, people.
in the teeth of it music,

acarrying on—breath.
Our pause mulls the made hills

and collected answer. before
happiness twirls on sticks we

see each other, look over
pattern and playtime.

that the whole waits
boggles.

time to go time to sit down
limits flower, breathing.

what seems often's a chorus—
breezes to see it, see to it—

is a way through life, ringing
laughter, hand.

what courses, baffles the to of it,
battles maleable, workable creation.

the thing made is a pause-shift
along the tideline.

a walk there to say hi to a friend
deriddles the singing earth.

cross search and dirt,
joy & orbit.

fill skirt with berries,
gravity, day.

what than to marry, limit to
smallest bounty. mouthfuls.

what than to mark hills
above the tree line—arrows

unto this last unpacked vowel.
act as one. be several

before sun and multiple seed.
pen notes to a future hello.

forget speed hurtles past
seated children, blind border.

forget hand, tools
and the thin but unlimited arc.

now, ground's clear. now begin
a courtship of blank justice.

whose heart's cured whose arc,
orbits in tiny bounty, sunlight.

simple empty undoes the last
marriage, child—alistening.

what powder, lint, wrinkle sits
waiting for light blue at a touch.

easy blooms ever memory.
felt heart, hill, arrows linger

pierce tiny diatom—
so, in miniature loss is nothing.

a leg, a word evaporates against
made horizon, unjust limit.

what makes it matter. the field
arcs to remedy blank will,

creation and an afternoon.
a band of shadow loosed, turned

round opinion, sentenced in
the quit and still equality.

trembling bigness in a thing.
point 1 to point 2 signals luck—
birds on strings, blank memory.

their wind and country send
a birthing self-city, wants.
burying ourselves in hinted
surroundings, we tiny it.

in a swerving limit you must
stop/start your life—migration
from melody to song and back.

in the shock of it love clenches
belly. how particular can we be
before it's all quaint, here before,
trembling together in it.

along the grassline, seed,
pattern.

before/after speaks—
forsythia again.

migration's enough for today.
evidence of no slight touch

marks the self-same heart
in vigil.

a cup sits there. relegates
hunches and guesswork

relegates aliving.
flattery shimmers overhead

until we see ourselves again.
it can be seen tuned to itself

whole, bellied and grown
in the green and greener.

chair, its curl and memory.
in it body draws circles,
city, tree, love from day—
aperture doubles.

undo a shoe, undo a war.
known-life begins as clicks of
true listening. block by block
we're here today,

faster 'til littlest fabric,
chair and false memory
renews surface, field,
or the just tucked into skin.

a blurb a secret recounted
confirms legs, their place in
field, current matter. there
is simple friendship,

a simple lover and the body
you love. its unknown flotsam,
its flocks turned face to face
in mid day sun

I can say I want you, tho
across your back's dispersant.

the sun did this to me. my
mind breaks from the

lyric ton, irresistable you—
medium of things and kiss.

so feed it the body you love
feed it the ferocious century.

I cannot become will not
be more than just simple

friend. no more questions
—interplay of mind. body is

here as I say your name
and kiss your face.

this is what to do together,
part encumbered part

manifest.

arrow marks root tree sky
arrow marks circular light.

before you others
held life on a string.

wind's here, in its blue blue.
medium of what to do

with the body you love. all
partly and all. the trick

plays out gene by gene, the
colored powder called ocean—

in it the body you love
bubbles.

so what pollen signifies
is not you or the soft blue

of memory or the use of it
to saturate limbed memory.

where you are now tosses
birds in air. the wind of which

tells stories witnesses can't recall
or pinpoint the whereabouts of

melody is time-boxed. the life of a line
mutes against blank justice til see is all
partly and all inside the body you love.
sing to form current, field, migration. it
doesn't get any better than the ferocious
century, the monuments ballooning miles
above the road.

cumulus and its unmatted future, a coursing
diatom, way to the store, all stutter. broken
line is a heart, forgiveness. dogwood flowers
disrupt light's continuity—traffick the same
remunerate body. ton by ton a mecca a gem's
dug miles above the road. this exhale confirms
gamete, twin, sets spots before our eyes.

severable life hills in us, swung, once life has
been done, then again flowered, lent symmetry.
everywhere currents of food and isolation. what
sex cuts back against kiss, pushes small freedom
to full. this particular measure, recurrent gift,
both cull and queue elemental nature, clematis,
measures a life at exhale.

there's a loop between life and after where
hands describe a circle in air. it canopies
the little things—its called barter and ethic.
there's life there for that ridiculous nature.

its future minutes us. each hello a vibrato,
bird litter, chirp: year or years totter— build,
built, building. the cumulus and unmatted is
upon us, its elemental measure an exhale.

dumb animal dumb reflection lifts the melody.
current migration trafficks the same remunerate
body, ton by ton. magic can't see the bird or seed
—plastic along the myriad stream of data.

still I see you. I can say I want you though
across your back's a filigree of work and sun.
it too a cut and shadow. the house's hum's
a mother, child, a way to interior understanding.

cannot to. cannot of or speak this shuttered umbra,
the body I love. cannot move faster than the day
tho it hurtles passed seated children, passed little
things and their ultimately severable life.

what-life, wilderness. what dawn, its smallness and our, our line
strung on with it. what flotsam, flock tours my kinness, walk.
without laughter I remove your head, place it on the body you
love. a way west, a way to the filigree of pleasure and shadow.

migration did this to me. an inside, a life of ridiculous nature.
the trembling bigness in a thing buries hinted surroundings,
powders blue ocean with a kiss. its chair, there, in looped loop,
the cumulus what—fear or flame or frame listen-ing.

without it, not just friend but family, little dots of dots recur,
sparse scent of equal, of, to. this hills in us a dusting, wind-
blown—that is if we could remember birds on strings, what
huddles seated children and their ultimately severable lives.

it mentions you, the to and of of it. the broken line's forgiven
your tense, its recurrent knot. through it we hurtle across self
and self. re-play now and then explains we, makes me duplicate—
its aperture-inducing past and future.

this can't be the way it is. can't be a node on cheek and neck.
forced through straw, the tiny it resurfaces the pollen of you.
where we plays still, mind between kissings slips. now, ground's
clear. now begins the courtship of blank justice.

to repeat ones-self, repeat a life. it too vibrato. the limited arc
limited luck of sitting in world. that knee is not thigh baffles
connectedness, stunts figure-ground.

there is bathing
    lot. lake.
        there is the body you love.

strawberries &
firefly.
        oh, that June / July repetition . . .

were we we or clutter
        contrail? stamina,
           —deep blue in a whole.

this couldn't rescind a life
        tho seems right. a rememory
        at ways of dying

        wind, being awake.
      alive at the too to of it.
        neck, node pushes

        through the straw as kissings slip
past us to the wide world again.

after you.
life lilts past.

to the hilt of reason
nothing but hills.

after everything, I only ask
resemblance. 2me.

pure experience tasks a true you.
stamina.

how wind undulates the stop / start,
life missing its pin.
kisses track along cheek and neck
and back.

day's a plenty fullering what.
relief skins, bumps—

a blending vibrato of knee and thigh.
connected at the hip, birth,
its fire and ensuing telemetry

what jot cells life, what circumstance.
melody stains. privileged litter.
if I could turn to you and say here
it's better I do.

this will have to do. chair, table.
feigned parry of fear, of hope's repeatable . . .

this can't be the way it is.
such water, such travel pours into matter. lot.

schedule of say trick, stick, dirt.

how well crisis articulates fancy on margin,
strips. what then do we do?

little dots escape me now. powder
ferocious century, clot the air,
are counted.

a power marks everything, mercenary.
corrupted, my hand crosses
your face and back in love, struggle

to be together, unworldly and all.

this life—

particulate sun floats around it.
together a tree turns, unwrapped—
    paper, to everything—to flame to.

we answers itself that way.
    whole, the rung and such.
        —end game of ending.

one kiss lets life unfold—
    nowwhere now here,
        my punctualis my sun, day.

our secrets lip/outline scatter.
    strip above-below.
        'til how who isn't is am.

running, palms backward,
filled with water at temperature—
    'til everyday thing's done

# ROOF BOOKS
## *the best in language since 1976*

### Recent & Selected Titles
• social patience by David Brazil. 136 p. $15.95

• THE PHOTOGRAPHER by Ariel Goldberg. 84 p. $15.95

• TOP 40 by Brandon Brown. 138 p. $15.95

• DEAD LETTER by Jocelyn Saidenberg. 98 p. $15.95

• THE MEDEAD by Fiona Templeton. 314 p. $19.95

• LYRIC SEXOLOGY VOL. 1 by Trish Salah. 138 p. $15.95

• INSTANT CLASSIC by erica kaufman  90 p. $14.95

• A MAMMAL OF STYLE by Kit Robinson
& Ted Greenwald. 96 p. $14.95

• VILE LILT by Nada Gordon. 114 p. $14.95

• DEAR ALL by Michael Gottlieb. 94 p. $14.95

• FLOWERING MALL by Brandon Brown. 112 p. $14.95.

• MOTES by Craig Dworkin. 88 p. $14.95

• APOCALYPSO by Evelyn Reilly. 112 p. $14.95

• BOTH POEMS by Anne Tardos. 112 p. $14.95

Roof Books are published by
Segue Foundation
300 Bowery • New York, NY 10012
For a complete list,
please visit roofbooks.com

Roof Books are distributed by
SMALL PRESS DISTRIBUTION
1341 Seventh Street • Berkeley, CA. 94710-1403.
spdbooks.org